First published in Great Britain 1985
English translation © J. M. Dent & Sons Ltd 1985
Originally published in German under the title
Rund ums Rad
© 1975, 1985 by Otto Maier Verlag, Ravensburg

Printed in Italy
ISBY 0 460 06229 8

The problem of transporting heavy objects is almost as old as mankind

ALI MITGUTSCH
ALL ABOUT WHEELS

Translated by Noel Simon

J. M. Dent & Sons Ltd
London & Melbourne

Over thousands of years man developed all kinds of ways of carrying things. But the wheel has proved by far the most practical and efficient invention.

One of the earliest methods of moving heavy or cumbersome objects was to roll them along on tree trunks or logs

The oldest drawing of a wheel dates from the time of the Sumerian civilization, 3500 BC

By the standards of the time this wheel was a masterly achievement

More sophisticated tools

made it possible

to improve the rollers

until finally the wheel evolved

The Wheel — an ancient invention

The first wheels were solid, made of sections of a tree trunk. These wooden wheels cracked in the heat and were very roughly shaped, so did not last long. The Sumerians, who lived for about four thousand years between the Tigris and the Euphrates, improved on the original design: they constructed a wheel in three separate parts. The sections were bound together with withies, which, besides holding the parts in place, also allowed sufficient movement to act as a simple spring. If one of the parts was damaged or broken it could easily be replaced.

afw, dile rim

brzo brzo.

willow rods were used as binding cord

A primitive type of wheel from the Middle East which is practically unchanged to this day

Another type of wheel used until recently in Switzerland

Different types of wheel were made in both Asia and Europe. They were adapted to a variety of uses. The wheel is already more than four thousand years old. How many modern inventions will still be in use a thousand years from now?

The wheel played an important part in the building of the Tower of Babel

3

Rollers and Treadmill

Sensible, lazy slave

The master-builder

Several keen slaves anxious to become assistant overseers

Two men fed-up with being slaves

The Pharaohs built monumental tombs and pyramids. Tens of thousands of slaves were engaged in their construction. Enormously heavy stones were moved on rollers to the building site, where they were laid in tiers. For such extremely heavy weights rollers were easier to use than wheels. As the huge load moved slowly forward, the hindmost log became free and was carried to the front. When heavy loads had to be lifted either on a building site or into a vessel in port, various types of wooden wheels were used. As there were, of course, no engines, the driving power came from people operating either inside or outside the wheel. These were known as treadmills.

Boring and poorly paid work

Mechanised crane

(Flanders, 16th century)

4

Chief overseer

Slave whip

A drummer who wasn't quick enough to get his leg out of the way of a roller

Drum for beating time

Slaves were employed in large gangs

These types of wheels were mainly used in the building of bridges and fortifications

Chariots

Egyptian hunting- and war-chariot from the reign of Pharoah Tutankhamen

The horse's harness was adorned with feathers and their coats ornamented with gold plate

The wheels were bronze

Driving a war-chariot called for constant practice and great skill

An Egyptian horse's elegant head-dress

Roman legionary in ceremonial armour

Celtic war-chariot

Roman combat- and war-chariot

Horse with Roman harness

This type of chariot was used by the Romans for both fighting and racing, as well as for carrying despatches and mail

Some of the types of carnivorous animals hunted and slaughtered by Egyptian potentates on their expeditions

A chariot for two, suitable for use on poor roads

A bronze Etruscan chariot with light wheels

Springs

Besides pursuing the enemy this war-chariot was almost equally dangerous to its driver who, besides fighting had also to control the horses and cling tight

Ancient bronze wheel

The Romans attached sharp sickle-like blades to the wheels to harass enemy infantry

The wounded were generally carried by hand

Wheeled Vehicles

Foot soldiers

Weapons

Wood and leather construction

This military vehicle is drawn by four asses

A Sumerian battle wagon from Ur, built in 2500 BC

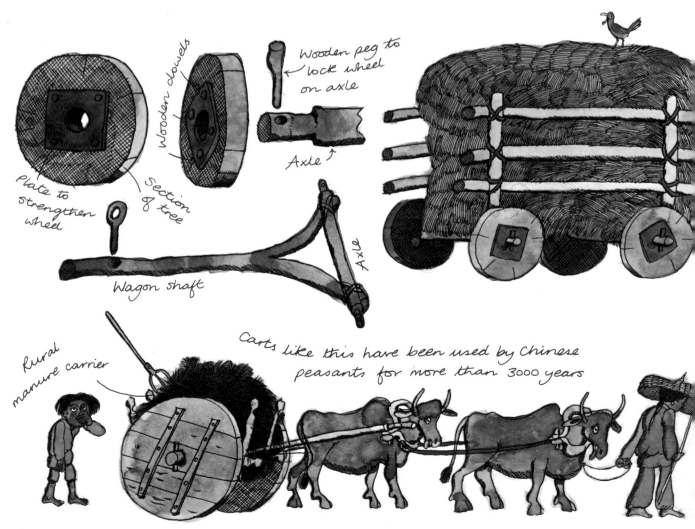

Plate to strengthen wheel

Wooden dowels

Section of tree

Wooden peg to lock wheel on axle

Axle →

Wagon shaft

Axle

Rural manure carrier

Carts like this have been used by Chinese peasants for more than 3000 years

There have always been people keen to conquer and pillage. After defeating an enemy or capturing a merchant, the survivors would be taken into slavery and either worked incredibly hard or sold. Here a slave caravan meets with an accident.

Typical merchandise

Fine cloth

Spices

Wine

Salt

Protective covering to keep off rain

Carter

Lockable metal money boxes

Protective straw bales

Rope

Transporting Merchandise over the Alps

Numerous merchants — such as this one from Nuremberg — traded between the ports of northern Italy and the principal cities of Europe. They hauled their wagons over alpine passes and through many small principalities and states.

They transported their merchandise on sturdy wagons and often travelled in convoy for mutual protection against the highwaymen, thieves and robbers who infested the roads.

As the rulers of the countries through which they passed levied road tolls and customs duty on all travellers, trading was a costly business.

It was also an extremely hazardous occupation. Apart from robbers and greedy rulers, the merchants had to contend with the dangers of bad weather and flooding. By the time the caravan reached its destination safely the traders had earned their profits — which, if all went well, could be substantial.

Musket

Armed guard

Robber's knife

Pistol

Highwayman

Customs duty had to be paid at the border crossing

Coins for paying to cross bridges and use roads

Customs officer - official highwayman!

Outrider

Up to twelve horses might be required to haul a wagon over steep and hazardous mountain passes

Iron rims

Uphill - supporting the wheel from behind

Early types of brakes

Downhill - the brake poles had to be frequently replaced

Brake shoes

The brakes locked against the rim

Regal Splendour

Rulers and powerful people travelled in splendid coaches. The[y] wanted to impress everybody with their own power and importance. In the ey[es] of the people such sumptuous displays served to confirm the authority and affluenc[e]

Items carried in the coach

Silks from the Orient ↑

Jewellery and ornaments of gold, silver and precious stones

A Viking noblewoman's richly ornamented bridal carriage and its contents

A European monarch's modest but rugged state coach, c. 1000 AD

← Sceptre

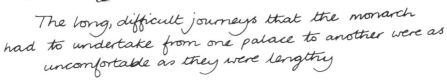

The long, difficult journeys that the monarch had to undertake from one palace to another were as uncomfortable as they were lengthy

A Persian princess's state carriage

Postilion

the state. The pomp
[an]d show of a royal
[pr]ocession so dazzled
[th]e onlooker that he
[w]as hardly aware of the
[o]ccupant of the
[ca]rriage. The power
[an]d splendour of the
[st]ate was symbolized by
[th]e coach, not by the
[ru]ler sitting inside it.

Coachman's seat covered
with richly embroidered velvet

Decorated springs

*The nose of his majesty King Ludwig II of Bavaria

Bodywork of leather and canvas

A Chinese mandarin's litter

The ass had to be led

During the bitter winters, 18th century travellers

Kept warm by wrapping themselves in thick furs and carrying charcoal braziers in the coach

The first heated caravan came from Russia

Besides passengers, coaches also carried mail

Abs. Joh. Maier

Sealing wax was used to seal letters

Carriages and Coaches

For centuries almost all transport was b
horse-drawn vehicles.

The Romans instituted a relay syster
which enabled ambassadors and other
important officials to travel quickly fror
Rome to distant provinces.

For hundreds of years bot
administrative and economi
development, as well as the
conveyance of passengers an
mail, relied on the horse.
In 1516 Emperor Charles V
established a comprehensive

...postal service based on horse-drawn vehicles. Relay stations were established at regular intervals throughout the realm where tired horses and coachmen could be exchanged for fresh ones. This system made it possible for people to travel surprisingly quickly.

A carriage, c.1300 AD

Post-horn

Even the nobility suffered accidents on the poor roads

At night it was often necessary for a man carrying a lantern to lead the way

Bad roads and hard wheels encouraged coach designers to invent springs

Light basket-work body

Coachman

The trusty horse

15

A rogues gallery of highwaymen over the centuries

Highway Robbery and Highwaymen

Long-distance travellers were always the prey of outlaws who made a living by robbing merchants and travellers of their valuables. The countryside was at one time infested with highwaymen who emerged from hideouts to fall upon wagon trains and caravans. Robber barons and their bands of desperados swept down from their castles and strongholds to rob and kill. For centuries nomadic tribesmen inhabiting the steppes and deserts regarded caravans as legitimate objects of plunder.

Several celebrated highwaymen — the best known among them being Robin Hood — have even been admired for claiming that they robbed the rich to give to the poor. Nowadays we have to cope with all kinds of terrorism including the hijacking of aircraft and the kidnapping and ransoming of hostages. So, even today it is still sometimes risky for wealthy people to travel.

Correct order of precedence from the most distinguished person to the humblest servant was considered vitally important

The favourite prey of the highwayman was an unguarded luxury coach

als Fargo stagecoach

ggage

Many men, either mounted or on foot, who attempted to hold up coaches and other wheeled traffic...

Executioner's cart

... took their last journey on wheels

17

Gunner in ceremonial uniform

Swab for cleaning gun barrel

Large powder keg

Length of fuse

Small cask

Ball ammunition and lead pellets

Iron cannon ball

Coat of arms

Wooden gun carriage

Metal clasps to strengthen the wood

Gunner's quadrant for estimating range

The horse remained man's chief helper until well into the 20th century

Iron-shod wheels were strong and durable

Bricks

Builder's cart...

Weapons on Wheels

Once gunpowder had been invented and its potential understood, the next step was to develop weapons with which to harness its destructive power. Ever larger gun barrels were cast, designed to fire iron or stone shot. The problem of controlling the cannon's violent recoil and returning it as quickly as possible to its firing position was met by mounting it on wheels.

Muzzle cap for keeping out rain and dust

Different kinds of cannon balls

stone

stone with iron bands

iron

Bomb

In the days when soldiers were rewarded with plunder, isolated houses well-to-do families were tempting targets

A wheelbarrow was frequently the most convenient way of transporting the wounded in the 15th century

former officer

Manservant or compassionate friend

and making mortar

Although the wheel contributed to the destruction of fortresses, villages and towns, it also aided their reconstruction. In recent times the development of wheeled vehicles specially designed for invalids has been instrumental in giving them unprecedented independence.

A self-propelled invalid chair, Nuremberg 1685

Hand crank

Cogged wheel

and trailer

19

Peddler

Bale of goods

Camel – the ship of the desert

Bedouin

White hunters

Eskimo dog-sled drawn by a team of huskies

Smugglers

papoose

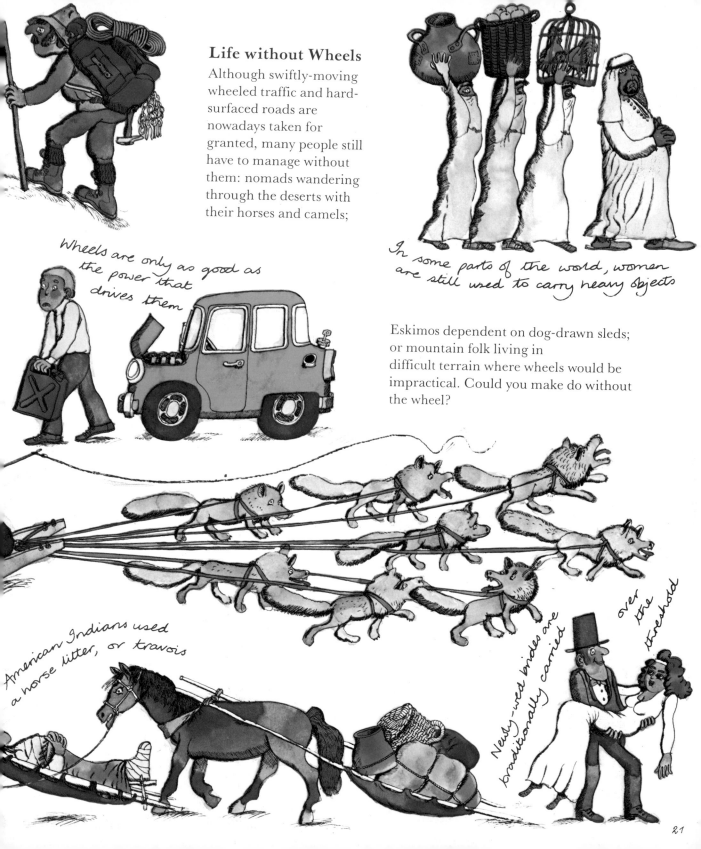

Life without Wheels

Although swiftly-moving wheeled traffic and hard-surfaced roads are nowadays taken for granted, many people still have to manage without them: nomads wandering through the deserts with their horses and camels;

Wheels are only as good as the power that drives them

In some parts of the world, women are still used to carry heavy objects

Eskimos dependent on dog-drawn sleds; or mountain folk living in difficult terrain where wheels would be impractical. Could you make do without the wheel?

American Indians used a horse litter, or travois

Newly-wed brides are traditionally carried over the threshold

21

A wind-propelled freight car with umbrella-like sails designed to catch the wind and pull the vehicle along

Sails on Wheels

The ancient Egyptians were the first to build a wind-powered vehicle, 4000 years ago. In the heyday of the sailing ship, numerous attempts were made to harness the wind for sailing on land. Four hundred years ago the Dutch engineer, Simon Stevin, built a land-sailer capable of carrying thirty people.

A budding wind-surfer →

A sail-buggy on rails

A thirty-man sailing wagon of 1600

This kite-drawn car proved unmana

Pennant

foresail

Whippet

A wind-propelled wagon first tried out on the beaches of Flanders

A lightly constructed wooden frame covered with silk

But it was not very efficient. Nor were attempts at 'sailing on wheels' any more successful.

Built by Simon Stevin

Sail-assisted wheelbarrow in Shanghai

Hacquet's 'Eolienne' cruising the streets of Paris, 1834

Observation platform used in fine weather

Helmsman

23

Transported by Muscle-power

The ability to move effortlessly is one of man's oldest ambitions. The challenge to devise some method of mechanical propulsion led inventive people to experiment with all kinds of self-propelled vehicles, based initially on muscle-power. This resulted in an infinite number of inventions as ingenious as they were fanciful. Of them all, the bicycle is the only one to have survived down to the present.

An all-wood vehicle

A primitive method of propulsion

A vehicle of about c.1420 relying on muscle-power aided by ropes and gears

Power was generated by hand cranking

The earliest known hobby horse, as pictured on a church window, about 1600

Cog wheels

Pedal-powered tricycle of c. 1800, with spring seat

This mechanically propelled vehicle was built at the beginning of the 16th century for the triumphal procession of the Emperor Maximilian

Wooden wheels

Stabilizer

Pedals

Decorative screw

Steering bar

Metal fork

Lantern could be hung here for driving at night

24

It would be reasonable to assume that man's ingenuity in devising new technology will continue to produce even more remarkable developments in the future.

A child's tricycle of c.1850

Hand crank

chain guard

The vehicle was richly figure decorated with carved scenes of events in the life of the emperor

Driver

Suitable for two passengers

Silver-handled cane

Powered by men cranking by hand both from inside the vehicle and from the rear

Footrest

tricycle

Tret-Motor-Wagen

Air-filled rubber tyres

Pedal-operated tricycle used by tradesmen for local deliveries

A conveyence similar to this, known as a 'cycle rickshaw', is used in parts of Asia to this day

A contemporary scene

25

Saddle

Dandy horse of 1818

Hobby horse of 1819

The Bicycle

The forerunner of the modern bicycle was the hobby horse, the dandy horse, and that aptly named velocipede, the boneshaker. In the middle of the last century wheels were developed with steel spokes and solid rubber tyres. The uneven, pot-holed roads of that time did not make cycling either pleasant or safe. Then came the invention of the chain-drive, transmitting power from the rear wheel, followed by John Boyd Dunlop's invention of the pneumatic tyre which helped make the bicycle a more comfortable and efficient machine. Mass-production has had the effect of reducing production costs until the bicycle is today the most popular and widely distributed conveyance in the world.

View of cycling school in a Viennese suburb, 1825

Hobby horse instructor

A fashionable conveyance in the middle of the 19th century was the penny-farthing. The cyclist was perched so high above the ground that mounting and dismounting was difficult, and sometimes dangerous.

no springs

Tra-la-la!

Reserve tank

An excursion on a bicycle-made-for-four

Solid rubber tyres

The unicycle was favoured by acrobats

American unicycle, patented in 1880. Recommended for keep-fit enthusiasts

Also used for performing on high wire

An up-and-coming cyclist

Safety bicycle of 1881 with double cogged gear

riding a the bicycle

The driver of this racing bike finds it an uphill struggle

Pneumatic tyres

Modern bicycle - the 'High-rise'

Wellspring front fork

Leather strap

Sheet metal

Cast-iron wheels

This one-footed German roller skate of 1879 had only two wheels, one behind the other

The first roller skate was of wood with iron rim...

Double-wheeled... and single-wheeled roller skates, late 19th century

The skater's waltz

Wooed by an ardent admirer

Plates strapped to the calves protect this skater's legs

Aspiring ladies' man

Wooden twin-wheeler

Elegant sporting types were great admi... the lad...

28

Roller-skating is certainly easier these days, with smoother streets and more sophisticated skates — but the first steps are still the most difficult.

The champion

The novice

Roller Skates

Roller skating was, and still is, a very popular sport. Once it has been mastered, skating gives the sensation of easy and almost effortless movement. Roller skating is not a very old sport. It became popular only after the appearance of smooth, level surfaces extensive enough for the purpose. Around the turn of the century indoor skating to the accompaniment of orchestral music became the vogue. In Berlin, Vienna and Paris it was fashionable to skate to work along the broad, tree-lined avenues. Today, it is once again an extremely popular amusement. There are roller skating contests and even a world championship.

Roller skating is much more fun today than it was when streets were cobbled and full of ruts and potholes

Belt

Spring-operated roller skate, 1923

Bending the leg automatically wound the spring

Mudguard

Steel spring

Steadying strap

Motorized skate, 1917

Dutch single mono-skate, 1920

Multi-wheeled roller skate

Contemporary skate

29

The first steam engine was built by Cugnot, in 1769

It travelled at a speed of 4 kph, but had to stop every quarter an 8 hour

Smokestack

Boiler

Stoke hole

Firebox

Drive-wheel

Hardwood construction

Steam Power

When water is heated to a sufficiently high temperature it is converted into steam. As steam has a greater volume than water, pressure builds up in a boiler. This pressure then generates the power to be capable, for instance, of activating the pistons of a locomotive.

Practically every type of mechanical vehicle — from automobile and motor-bike to steam roller and locomotive — has evolved from a steam-driven forerunner.

Powerful brakes

Steam roller

An early steam kettle

Steam carriage used for public transport

Stoker

Model steam engine

Whistle

Safety valve

Patented by John Squire, 1883

first steam-powered bicycle, 1870

Drive belt

Steam driven amphibious vehicle

Designed to travel on both land and water

Waterwheel

Wheels for travelling on land

'Steam Carriage' 1834

Boiler

Safety valve

Light master

Searchlight vehicle made by Siemens

Light operator

Searchlight

Horse-drawn

Electric cables

Used for illuminating sports arenas, etc.

The steam train revolutionized transportation to an extent that influenced the development of almost every country in the world. It linked neighbouring countries with one another and opened up remote regions such as the vast expanses of Siberia and the sparsely settled West in America. The railways system, which quickly developed in all continents, brought the nations of the world closer together.

George Stephenson's 'Rocket', 1829

steam regulator

Cylinder

Smokestack

Bumper

Water

Coal

Coupling

In England, a man carrying a red warning flag had to walk ahead of every steam vehicle

Firebox

Drive wheel

The 'Eagle', 1835

The first German train, which operated between Nuremberg and Fürth

Open carriages

Wood-burning American locomotive, 1860, with spark guard and cow-catcher

Locomotive and saloon car of the Khedive of Egypt, 1859

Postal wagon, 1910

Steam locomotive

Coal tender

Electric train

Streamlined styling

The so-called 'wheeled zeppelin' was propeller driven

attains a speed of 210 - 240 Kph

The fastest train in the world travels between Tokyo and Osaka a

Shot horses

Wounded

Marksmen

Chiefs

The railway brought ever increasing numbers of settlers
armed with superior weapons and equipment into conflict
with the Indians. The railroad, which the Indians
named 'iron horse', played a decisive role in opening up
and winning the Wild West and in taking land away from
its original inhabitants.

From Petrol-driven Carriage to Automobile

The automobile was the natural successor to the carriage. The invention of the steam engine was followed by the idea of building a carriage which could move independently of horse- or man-power. This led to the development of the steam coach and, later, the automobile. In Germany in 1885 Carl Benz constructed a petrol-driven carriage equipped with an internal combustion engine designed by Nikolaus August Otto. The first engine-driven vehicle was called a 'petrol carriage'.

Within a surprisingly short time the petrol carriage was followed by a carefully designed street vehicle. The first automobiles were, of course, hand-made. Because they were expensive, only the well-to-do could afford them.

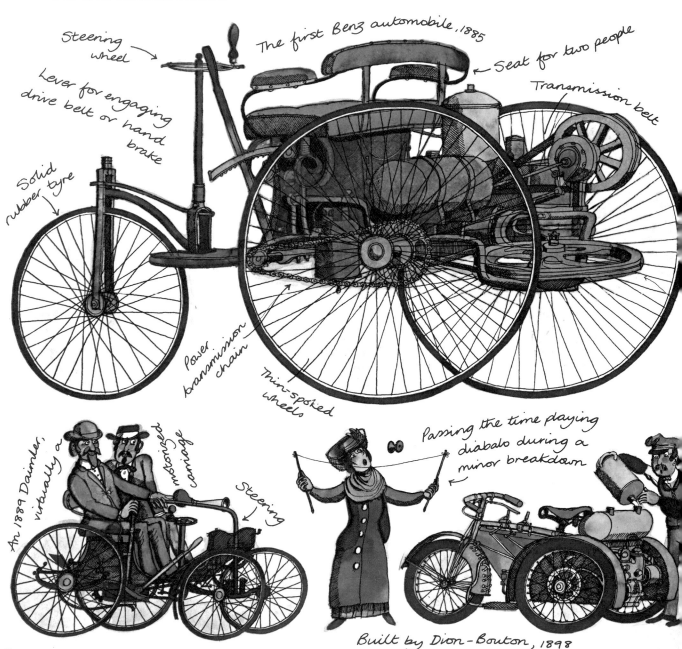

Steering wheel

The first Benz automobile, 1885

Seat for two people

Lever for engaging drive belt or hand brake

Transmission belt

Solid rubber tyre

Power transmission chain

Thin-spoked wheels

An 1889 Daimler, virtually a motorized carriage

Steering

Passing the time playing diabolo during a minor breakdown

Built by Dion-Bouton, 1898

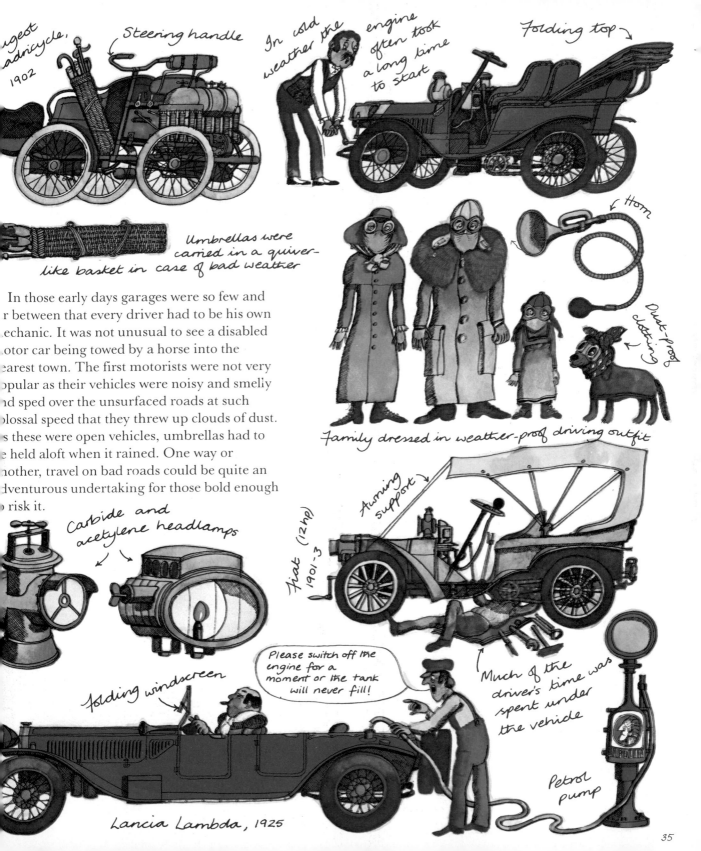

...ugeot
...adricycle,
1902

Steering handle

In cold weather the engine often took a long time to start

Folding top

Umbrellas were carried in a quiver-like basket in case of bad weather

Horn

Dust-proof clothing

Family dressed in weather-proof driving outfit

In those early days garages were so few and ...r between that every driver had to be his own ...echanic. It was not unusual to see a disabled ...otor car being towed by a horse into the ...earest town. The first motorists were not very ...opular as their vehicles were noisy and smelly ...nd sped over the unsurfaced roads at such ...olossal speed that they threw up clouds of dust. ...s these were open vehicles, umbrellas had to ...e held aloft when it rained. One way or ...nother, travel on bad roads could be quite an ...dventurous undertaking for those bold enough ...o risk it.

Carbide and acetylene headlamps

Fiat (12hp) 1901-3

Awning support

Much of the driver's time was spent under the vehicle

folding windscreen

Please switch off the engine for a moment or the tank will never fill!

Petrol pump

Lancia Lambda, 1925

Henry Ford's design studio

Mass-production

The diversity of styles and types in the early days of the automobile was astonishing. Most cars were built to order. Not only was the bodywork individually designed, with great attention paid to good fashioning and elegant lines, but the interiors were luxuriously equipped, and the engines themselves were almost works of art. Not many people could afford them.

In 1908, Henry Ford designed and built the famous Model T. Ford had studied conveyorbelts and overhead trolley systems in meat-packing factories. He was the first to use these systems in a car factory to move the parts to their assembly points. As Model T's could be built much faster than other cars Ford was able to lower the price to bring them within the reach of almost everybody.

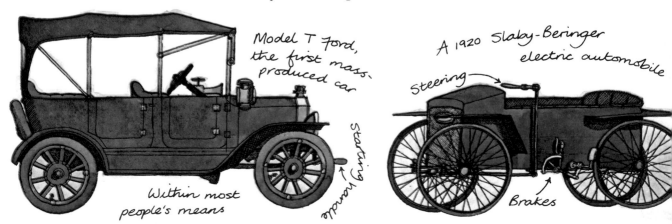

Model T Ford, the first mass-produced car

Within most people's means

starting handle

A 1920 Slaby-Beringer electric automobile

steering

Brakes

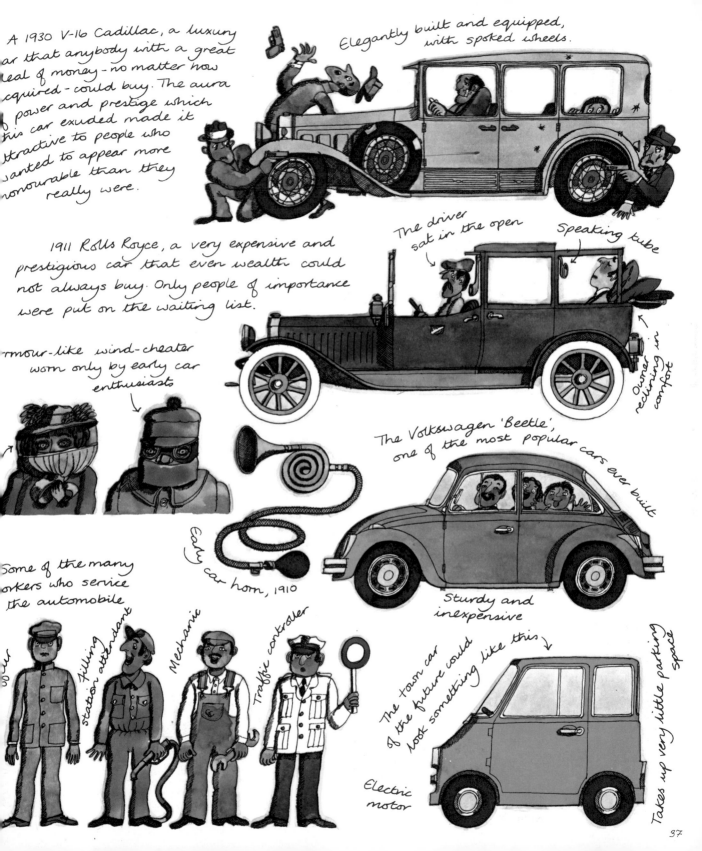

A 1930 V-16 Cadillac, a luxury car that anybody with a great deal of money - no matter how acquired - could buy. The aura of power and prestige which this car exuded made it attractive to people who wanted to appear more honourable than they really were.

Elegantly built and equipped, with spoked wheels.

1911 Rolls Royce, a very expensive and prestigious car that even wealth could not always buy. Only people of importance were put on the waiting list.

The driver sat in the open

Speaking tube

Owner reclining in comfort

Armour-like wind-cheater worn only by early car enthusiasts

The Volkswagen 'Beetle', one of the most popular cars ever built

Early car horn, 1910

Sturdy and inexpensive

Some of the many workers who service the automobile

Driver

Filling station attendant

Mechanic

Traffic controller

The town car of the future could look something like this

Electric motor

Takes up very little parking space

37

Early fire fighters had to rely on a chain of people passing buckets of water by hand

Primitive fire engine

operated by two to eight people

Pump operator

Nightwatch man rudely awakened from his midday siesta

Jumping sheet

A New York fire engine of 1853 reacting to an alarm

Fire Fighting

As soon as the alarm is raised the fire brigade must get to the scene of the fire with all speed. Powerful fire extinguishers and fire fighting appliances have to be taken to the site. Fire brigades have always been quick to adapt improved transport to their own specialized requirements. This led to the development of the

As buildings grew taller, ladders had to be correspondingly longer

Extremely powerful pump

No. 15

A typical modern fire engine

ingenious hand-operated pump. As well as working the pump themselves, the firemen had to haul their own fire engine. Later, horses were used. These were followed by engine-driven pumps carried on motor vehicles. But as towns and cities grew the problems of rescuing people from blazing buildings became greater. Among the better recent developments are easily movable swivel-mounted platforms, hydraulically operated ladders, powerful hoses and water cannon.

The Dennis fire engine used in London from 1914 until the Second World War

Alarm bell

The 'Elephant', a horse-drawn fire engine with steam-operated pump, used in New York in the 1850s. The fire took so long to kindle that the boiler had to be kept permanently alight.

The hose cart had to be pulled by hand

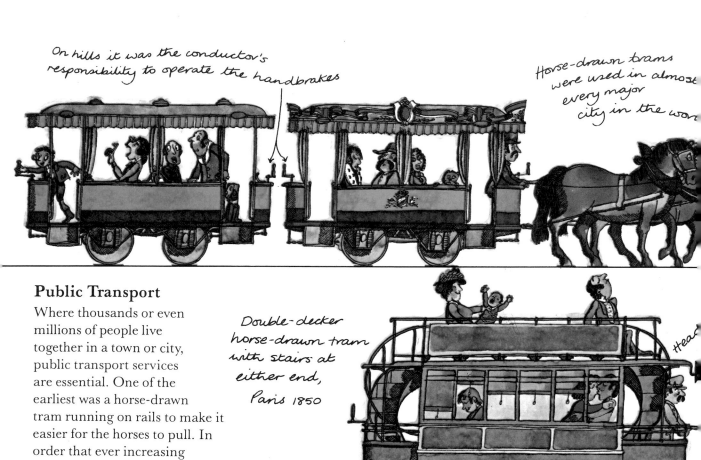

On hills it was the conductor's responsibility to operate the handbrakes

Horse-drawn trams were used in almost every major city in the wor...

Public Transport

Where thousands or even millions of people live together in a town or city, public transport services are essential. One of the earliest was a horse-drawn tram running on rails to make it easier for the horses to pull. In order that ever increasing numbers of people could use the system, additional coaches were added either behind or on top of one

Double-decker horse-drawn tram with stairs at either end, Paris 1850

Head...

Running board →

Passengers could travel first, second or third class, with fares priced accordingly

Smokestack

'Santiago Coruña', one of the earliest steam buses buil... at the turn of the century, ha... a large luggag... rack on the roof.

Canvas and wood

another. But the real breakthrough in public transport came with the electrification of the tramways and the installation of petrol engines in buses. Today, the demand for expensive public transport is largely met by underground electric trains and diesel-engined buses. Bus and train fares, especially in the sprawling cities of the third world, are a heavy burden on the poorer section of the population. In the richer countries public transport is often relatively expensive and thus little used. Many people prefer to travel everywhere in their own cars, thereby crowding the roads with traffic.

Steam omnibus, 1840

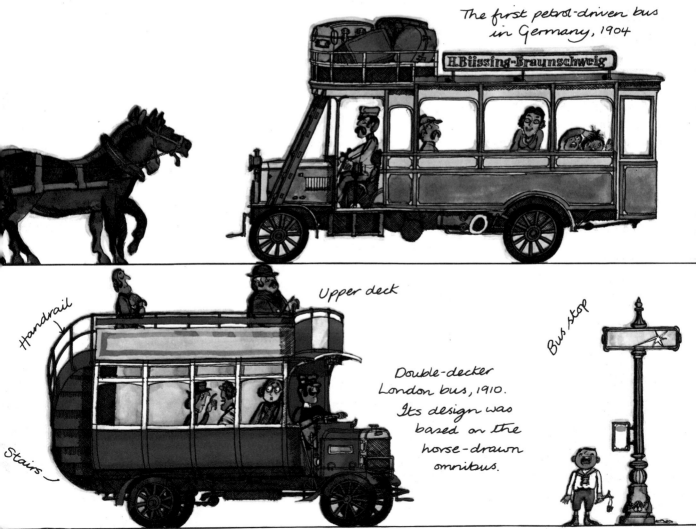

The first petrol-driven bus in Germany, 1904

H.Büssing-Braunschweig

Upper deck

Handrail

Stairs

Bus stop

Double-decker London bus, 1910. Its design was based on the horse-drawn omnibus.

The first rail-less freight train, built in 1903 by Joseph Vollmer

GRAND HOTEL

Delivery cart for wines and spirits

Snow plough

Mobile shopping trolley

Container lorry

42

Freight Carriers and other Useful Vehicles

Nowadays an immense variety of wheeled vehicles has been designed to meet our every need. It is impossible to imagine life without them. The raw materials, food, fuel, manufactured goods, and all the other things needed for day-to-day living, are carried on wheels. Indeed, civilized life as we know it would be almost unthinkable without that simple, age-old invention, the wheel.

Bulldozer for earth shifting and heavy construction work

Exhaust

Travelling bear cage

Circus tractor

Electric baggage train used at airports and railway stations

Go-cart

Electric golf caddie

Multi-purpose vehicle for travelling on both land and sea

Amphibious car

Propeller

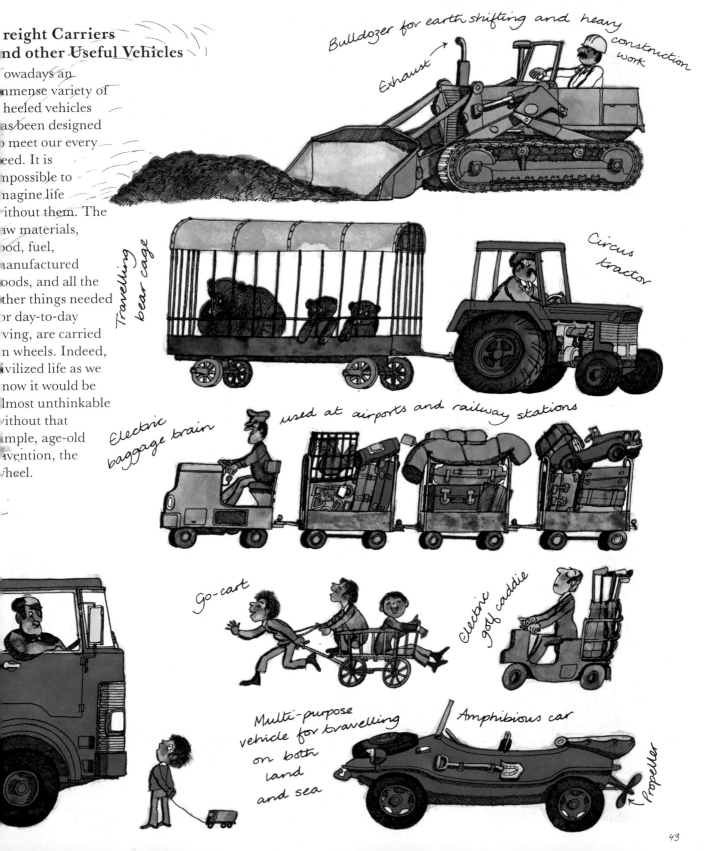

Milestones in Motor Racing

Blitzen Benz, 1911 (200 hp)

Soap box

1910–1911 Fiat (300 hp)

Hardly had the automobile been invented than men began to race it faster and faster. In 1906 the speed record already stood at 205 kph; by 1911 this had been increased to 228 kph.

Opel Rocket Car, RAK 2.

Attained a speed of 220 kph in Berlin, 1928

OPEL RAK 2

1954 Mercedes Benz, the 'Silver Arrow'

Capable of 400 kph.

Pit crewman with lap board

+5 Peter T 18

Starter

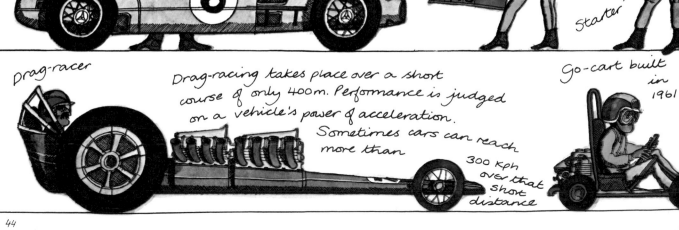

Drag-racer

Drag-racing takes place over a short course of only 400 m. Performance is judged on a vehicle's power of acceleration. Sometimes cars can reach more than 300 kph over that short distance

Go-cart built in 1961

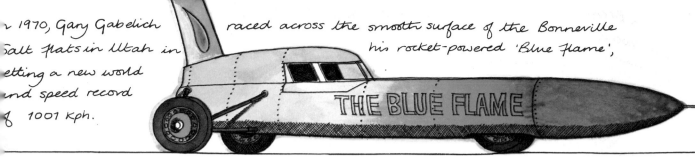

In 1970, Gary Gabelich raced across the smooth surface of the Bonneville Salt Flats in Utah in his rocket-powered 'Blue Flame', setting a new world land speed record of 1001 Kph.

THE BLUE FLAME

Lotus 72

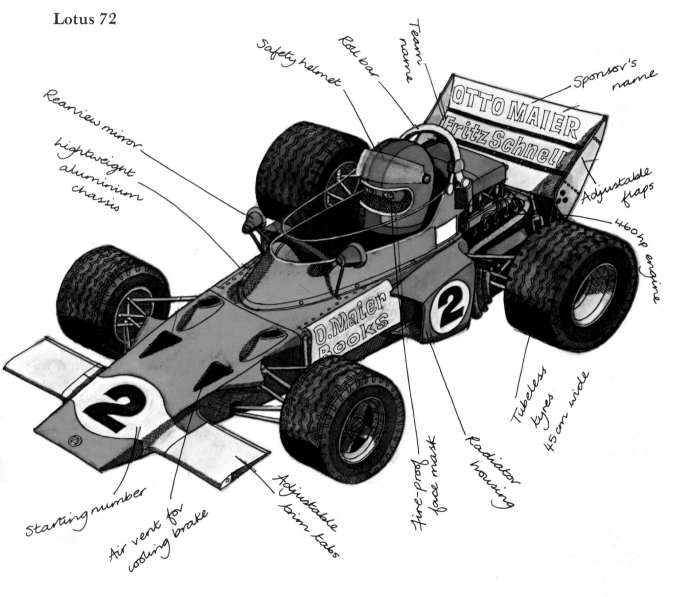

Team name

Roll bar

Safety helmet

Sponsor's name

OTTO MAIER

Fritz Schnell

Adjustable flaps

Rearview mirror

Lightweight aluminium chassis

460 hp engine

D.Maier Books

2

2

Tubeless tyres 45 cm wide

Starting number

Air vent for cooling brake

Adjustable trim tabs

Fire-proof face mask

Radiator housing